W9-BGU-223

Date: 12/16/16

J BIO MONROE
Kelley, K. C.,
James Monroe : the 5th president

A FIRST LOOK AT
AMERICA'S PRESIDENTS

JAMES MONROE

The 5th President

by K.C. Kelley

Consultants:
Philip Nash, Associate Professor of History
Pennsylvania State University
Sharon, Pennsylvania

Soo Chun Lu, Associate Professor of History
Indiana University of Pennsylvania
Indiana, Pennsylvania

BEARPORT
PUBLISHING

New York, New York

Credits

Cover, Courtesy White House; 4, Courtesy Artnc.org; 5, Courtesy Daderot/National Portrait Gallery/Wikimedia; 6, © Sue Ashe/Dreamstime; 7BL, © Ken Backer/Dreamstime; 7BR, Courtesy Washington and Lee University/Charles Peele/Wikimedia; 8, Courtesy Wikimedia/Metropolitan Museum of Art/painting by Emanuel Leutzke; 10, Courtesy White House Historical Association; 11T, Courtesy White House; 12, U.S. Naval History and Heritage Command Photograph; 13T, Courtesy National Archives; 13B, Courtesy White House Historical Association; 14, © Aiisha/Dollar Photo; 15T, © Everett Historical/Shutterstock; 15B, © North Wind Pictures Archives/Alamy; 16, © Markus Sipa/Dreamstime; 17L, © The James Monroe Museum; 17R, © C. Harrison Conroy Co., Inc.; 18, © Jbdodane/Alamy; 19T, © Design Pics, Inc./Alamy; 19B, © Americanspirit/Dreamstime; 20T, Courtesy White House Historical Association; 20B, Courtesy Wikimedia/Yale University Art Gallery; 21T, Courtesy White House; 21B, U.S. Naval History and Heritage Command Photograph; 22, Courtesy of College of William & Mary.

Publisher: Kenn Goin
Editor: Jessica Rudolph
Creative Director: Spencer Brinker
Production and Photo Research: Shoreline Publishing Group LLC

Library of Congress Cataloging-in-Publication Data

Names: Kelley, K. C., author.
Title: James Monroe : the 5th president / by K.C. Kelley ; consultants:
   Philip Nash, Associate Professor of History, Pennsylvania State University
   and Soo Chun Lu, Associate Professor of History, Indiana University of
   Pennsylvania.
Description: New York, New York : Bearport Publishing Company, Inc., 2017. |
   Series: A first look at America's presidents | Includes bibliographical
   references and index. | Audience: Ages 6–10.
Identifiers: LCCN 2016020327 (print) | LCCN 2016020911 (ebook) | ISBN
   9781944102647 (library binding) | ISBN 9781944997342 (ebook)
Subjects: LCSH: Monroe, James, 1758–1831—Juvenile literature. |
   Presidents—United States—Biography—Juvenile literature.
Classification: LCC E372 .K453 2017 (print) | LCC E372 (ebook) | DDC
   973.5/4092 [B] —dc23

LC record available at https://lccn.loc.gov/2016020327

For more information, write to Bearport Publishing Company, Inc., 45 West 21st Street, Suite 3B, New York, New York 10010. Printed in the United States of America.

10 9 8 7 6 5 4 3 2 1

CONTENTS

An Active American

James Monroe worked his entire life to serve the American people. When he was a young soldier, he fought to free America from British rule. As a politician, he helped form a new government. When he became president, Monroe worked to make the young nation strong.

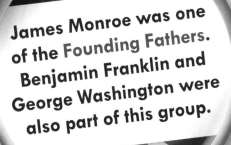

James Monroe was one of the Founding Fathers. Benjamin Franklin and George Washington were also part of this group.

Benjamin Franklin

James Monroe was
the fifth president.
He served from
1817 to 1825.

Life on the Farm

James Monroe was born in 1758. He lived on a farm in Virginia. His family owned slaves who worked on the farm. James spent his time going to school and hunting.

James's family grew tobacco on their farm.

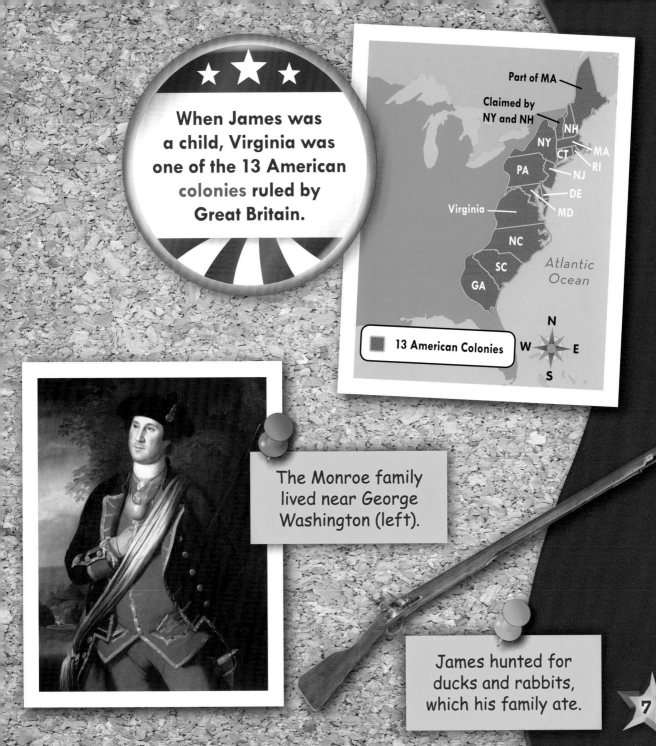

When James was a child, Virginia was one of the 13 American colonies ruled by Great Britain.

Part of MA

Claimed by NY and NH

NH

NY

CT

MA

RI

PA

NJ

DE

Virginia

MD

NC

Atlantic Ocean

SC

GA

N

W

E

S

13 American Colonies

The Monroe family lived near George Washington (left).

James hunted for ducks and rabbits, which his family ate.

In the Army

In 1775, when Monroe was 16 years old, the Revolutionary War broke out. The American colonies wanted to be free from Britain. Monroe joined the army and became an assistant to General George Washington. In 1776, Monroe was wounded in battle but recovered.

Washington

Monroe

In 1776, American soldiers crossed a river to attack enemy forces in New Jersey. In a famous painting of this event, Monroe is shown standing behind General Washington.

Serving in Government

After the Americans won the war in 1783, Monroe wanted to help the new country. He served as a U.S. **Senator** and then as **governor** for the state of Virginia. Monroe also worked with presidents George Washington and Thomas Jefferson.

In 1786, Monroe married Elizabeth Kortright.

Monroe worked with President Thomas Jefferson to buy land from France. The Louisiana Purchase of 1803 doubled the size of the United States.

Thomas Jefferson

Louisiana Territory

Pacific Ocean

Atlantic Ocean

N
W · E
S

The land that France sold to the United States was called the Louisiana Territory.

United States, 1803
Louisiana Territory
Today's border of the United States

11

War Again

In 1811, Monroe became part of President James Madison's **cabinet**. Monroe gave advice to the president on important matters. In 1812, America went to war with Britain once again. Monroe helped deal with Britain and plan how the war was fought. In 1815, the Americans won the war.

Many battles in the War of 1812 were fought at sea.

British troops attacked Washington, DC, in 1814. Monroe helped move government papers, including the U.S. Constitution, out of the city for safekeeping.

We the People

Article 1

When British soldiers attacked Washington, DC, they set fire to the White House.

Good Feelings

In 1816, Monroe ran for president and won. When he was president, new states became part of the nation, including Illinois and Alabama. Monroe helped Americans travel to these new lands by building **canals** and roads. The country was becoming bigger and stronger. People called this time the **Era** of Good Feelings.

In the early 1800s, people traveled by horse, horse-drawn carriage, or boat.

The Erie Canal was built in New York while Monroe was president.

In 1820, Monroe signed the Missouri Compromise. The law allowed slavery in new southern lands but banned it in new northern lands.

The Monroe Doctrine

In the 1820s, many European colonies in North and South America wanted their freedom. Monroe supported them. In 1823, he announced the Monroe **Doctrine**. It said America wouldn't let European countries set up new colonies in the region. It also stated that America would stay out of Europe's business.

The Monroe Doctrine included the entire Western Hemisphere, which is half of the earth.

Monroe signed the Monroe Doctrine at this desk.

As president, Monroe wore old-fashioned short pants and buckled shoes, which were popular in the 1770s.

17

Remembering Monroe

James Monroe died on Independence Day, July 4, 1831. He had worked hard to make the United States a free and strong nation. Today, Monroe is remembered as someone who spent his life serving the nation he loved.

Many cities are named after James Monroe.
Monrovia (above) is the capital of Liberia, a nation in Africa.

18

Two other presidents died on July 4. They were John Adams and Thomas Jefferson, who both passed away in 1826.

At Monroe's family home in Virginia, visitors can see what life was like in colonial times.

19

TIMELINE

Here are some major events from James Monroe's life.

1758
James Monroe is born in Westmoreland County, Virginia.

1775
The Revolutionary War begins.

1786
Monroe marries Elizabeth Kortright.

 1760   1770   1780   1790

1776
Monroe is wounded in the Battle of Trenton.

1790
Monroe becomes a U.S. Senator.

1816
Monroe is elected president.

1799
Monroe is elected governor of Virginia.

1823
Monroe announces the Monroe Doctrine.

1800

1810

1820

1830

1803
Monroe helps arrange the Louisiana Purchase.

1812
The War of 1812 begins.

1820
Monroe is elected to a second term.

1831
Monroe dies on July 4, at age 73.

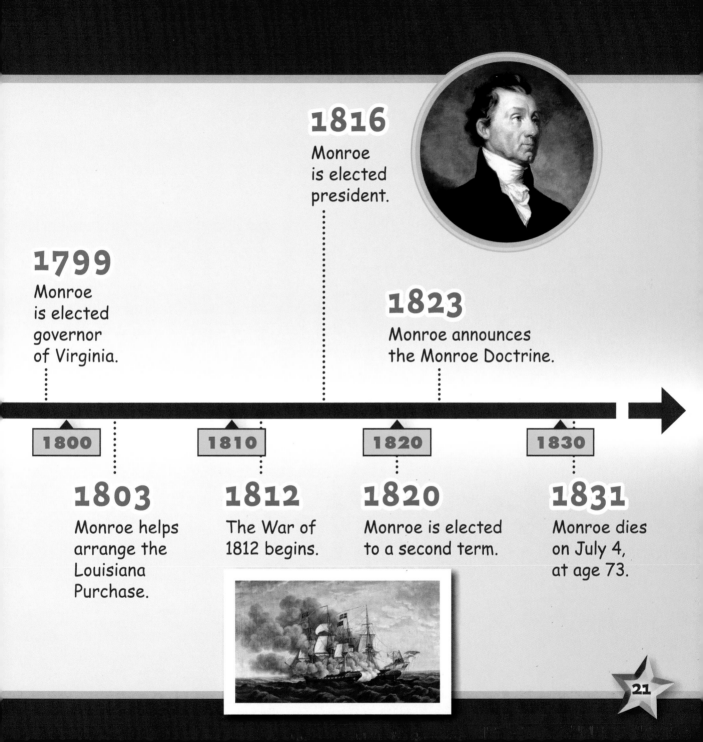

"We should consider any attempt on [Europe's] part to extend their system to any portion of this hemisphere as dangerous to our peace and safety."

In 1789, Monroe bought a farm in Virginia that was next door to Thomas Jefferson's home.

"The best form of government is that which is most likely to prevent the greatest sum of evil."

Monroe was the last president to have fought in the Revolutionary War.

22

GLOSSARY

cabinet (KAB-uh-net) the people chosen by a president to give advice

canals (kuh-NALZ) human-made waterways

colonies (KOL-uh-neez) areas that have been settled by people from another country and are ruled by that country

doctrine (DOK-trihn) an official statement of a government policy

era (AIR-uh) a long period of time

Founding Fathers (FOUND-ing FAHTH-urz) men who wrote documents, such as the U.S. Constitution, to create the United States

governor (GUV-ur-nur) the leader of a state

senator (SEN-uh-tur) a member of the lawmaking body of government

Index

Read More

Livi, Julia. *Let's Visit James Monroe!* Fredericksburg, VA: University of Mary Washington Foundation (2015).

Stabler, David. *Kid Presidents: True Tales of Childhood from America's Presidents*. Philadelphia: Quirk Books (2014).

Venezia, Mike. *James Monroe: Fifth President, 1817–1825*. New York: Children's Press (2005).

Learn More Online

To learn more about James Monroe, visit
www.bearportpublishing.com/AmericasPresidents

About the Author:
K.C. Kelley has written many biographies for young readers, including books about Betsy Ross, the Wright Brothers, and Milton Hershey.